FRANKLIN PARK PUBLIC LIBRARY

3 1316 00064 0907

D1489501

WITHDRAWN

FRANKLIN PARK PUBLIC LIBRARY
FRANKLIN PARK, IL.

Each borrower is held responsible for all library
material drawn on his card and for fines accruing on
the same. No material will be issued until such fine
has been paid.

All injuries to library material beyond reasonable
wear and all losses shall be made good to the
satisfaction of the Librarian.

WITHDRAWN

IT'S ECOLOGY

By DAVID GEORGE

Illustrated by MARCIN PIWOWARSKI

CANTATA
LEARNING

MANKATO, MINNESOTA

FRANKLIN PARK LIBRARY
FRANKLIN PARK, IL

CANTATA
LEARNING
MANKATO, MINNESOTA

Published by Cantata Learning
1710 Roe Crest Drive
North Mankato, MN 56003
www.cantatalearning.com

Copyright © 2015 Cantata Learning

All rights reserved. No part of this publication may be reproduced
in any form without written permission from the publisher.

Library of Congress Control Number: 2014938313
978-1-63290-080-7 (hardcover/CD)
978-1-63290-343-3 (paperback/CD)
978-1-63290-395-2 (paperback)

It's Ecology by David George
Illustrated by Marcin Piwowarski

Book design by Tim Palin Creative
Music produced by Wes Schuck
Audio recorded, mixed, and mastered at Two Fish Studios, Mankato, MN

Printed in the United States of America.

VISIT
WWW.CANTATALEARNING.COM/ACCESS-OUR-MUSIC

J577
GEO
64-0907

Ecology is the study of how living things relate to each other and what is around them. Ecologists research everything from tiny **organisms**, such as bacteria, to entire **habitats**, such as tropical rain forests. An **ecosystem** is a group of living things that exist in a particular area. Every living thing is part of an ecosystem.

It sounds so complicated. But we are all **related**, from the grass on the ground to the creatures all around and everything in between.

Long ago in a rain forest, you might have seen a big brontosaurus. Now they're gone, and others live on, you see.

From the fish in the sea in the Great Barrier Reef to the desert sands or in the grasslands, that's where we'll find life of all kinds. You see, it's ecology.

The **food chain** is all connected. Everything has been selected from the **fungus** that's among us to the birds that fly above us and everything in between.

We know a hawk can eat a snake, and a snake can eat a frog that's basking in the sun, lying on a log. And down around that tree are bugs the frog can eat. The bugs flying around are feeding on the peat. The peat starts to grow when that tree becomes old. We see, that's ecology.

Now we know about this story and ecology and all its glory. The world that we all see from the tigers and the trees and everything in between.

We know that all things come and go. And history will show that everything around goes back into the ground.

As things start to grow in the wetlands and the snow, we see, it's all ecology.

GLOSSARY

ecology—the study of how living things relate to one another and where they live

ecosystem—a group of living things that live in a particular area

food chain—a system of living things in which each member is eaten in turn by another living thing

fungus—a group of flowerless plants, such as mushrooms, that feed on dead things

habitat—the place where a living thing naturally lives and grows

organism—a living thing

related—belonging to the same family, group, or kind

It's Ecology

David George

Folk

ACTIVITY QUESTIONS:

1. Describe the ecosystem in which you live. What are some of the other organisms that share it with you? How do you relate to one another?

2. Design your own original ecosystem. What would it be like? Who would live in it? How would they relate to one another? What would the food chain look like?

TO LEARN MORE

Kessler, Colleen. *Hands-On Ecology: Real-Life Activities for Kids*. Waco, TX: Prufrock Press, 2006.

Aloian, Molly and Bobbie Kalman. *Rainforest Food Chains*. New York: Crabtree Publishing Company, 2006.

Salas, Laura Purdie. *Coral Reefs: Colorful Underwater Habitats*. Minneapolis, MN: Picture Window Books, 2009.

Salas, Laura Purdie. *Deserts: Thirsty Wonderlands*. Minneapolis, MN: Picture Window Books, 2007.

1361001